HOW TO GET REALLY GOOD AT FRENCH

Learn French to Fluency and Beyond

1st Edition

POLYGLOT LANGUAGE LEARNING

TABLE OF CONTENTS

PART ONE

Accelerated Language Learning

LEARN LIKE A POLYGLOT

W hen it comes to learning foreign languages, people want to learn fast. They want to save time. People want quick results, and they want to be able to speak fluently in a short amount of time.

But how long does it take to become fluent in French? The answer depends on your definition of the word "fluent" as well as your personal goals. Are you looking to visit a French speaking country and learn a handful of words and phrases before departing? Do you want to be able to hold a basic conversation with strangers in French? Is your plan to work a job that requires French proficiency at the professional level? When you understand how to learn a language fast and effectively, you will be able to meet all of those goals and go even further than you had previously imagined.

Faster language learning methods and techniques do exist, and they can help you get to your goals exponentially faster. To find these techniques and strategies, polyglots or people who speak several languages can offer us some important insight. Interviews, news stories, and viral videos with millions of views make these people out to be language geniuses, but if we look more closely at their stories rather than their abilities, there is an even more interesting truth. They often struggle intensely in learning their first foreign language, but something finally clicks within the gears of their minds. They learn that first one and go on to easily learn three, four, or even more.

Also, they all ditched school as a means to learn a language. Foreign language classes teach you about specific languages, but they do not teach you how to learn a foreign language. After lectures and lengthy explanations, you are left to your own study devices to memorize and absorb massive amounts of information in your head. We don't know any better as first time language learners, so we memorize vocabulary and phrase lists, do workbooks, reread old passages, and repeatedly listen to the same audio tracks found in our coursebook CDs. It can be extremely boring at times and expensive as well, but if you are studious enough, you will finish and graduate.

Even upon graduation, you will find that school does not teach us how to train our minds to understand the speed, speech patterns, and the different vocabulary that native speakers use in real life. Ask someone who majored in a foreign language in college what happened after they finally traveled or moved to the foreign country. You will hear a common tale that goes something like this. They asked for directions for the first time, and a lengthy reply was given. Nods and thank yous were exchanged, but just one or two words were understood.

Why People Fail in
Learning a New Language

Most polyglots weren't always good at learning foreign languages. It's a skill that they develop with each new language they take on. This is why the first one can be such a challenge for everybody. Without that language learning skill and experience, trying to learn and memorize thousands of French words, phrases, and grammar structures can seem like the ultimate test. And then, native speakers spit all of this out at seemingly a bazillion words a minute. It certainly sounds like a lot of hard work and study will be needed.

It's hard to argue against the value of hard work. It creates high-quality results. It pushes people to do what they need to do. It gets things done. But in the case of learning a foreign language, hard work can be misleading.

Beginning language learners might put themselves through hell to learn all of this information. They might try to learn a language like they studied in school. Old-fashioned study methods worked back then, so why can't it work now? Rereading, rewriting, and re-listening to the same vocabulary, sentences, dialogues, and short stories are not very effective means to memorize new language in the long term. They are also tedious and not very fun ways to learn.

These simple methods may put new words into your short-term memory, but if you hope to be a fluent French speaker one day, you'll need to store these words into your long-term memory and be able to recall them with ease. You'll need to recognize them whenever they are spoken during conversation or used in written text. All of this is possible and easy to achieve with more fun and effective language learning techniques.

Flashcards are a common tool for learning new words, but they are not the most exciting option when taken at face value. A very common type that you might find will put an English word on the front side of these cards and test us on our ability to recall the equivalent French word which is on the back side. While these basic flashcards can be useful, it can be difficult to keep your attention on these exercises past the 5-10 minute mark. In this book, we will look at a variety of exercises that will help to maximize your attention span and see if we can make the learning process a bit more fast-paced and enjoyable.

Some exercises can be taken to frustrating levels of difficulty with the intention to learn faster. These often have the opposite effect. For instance, you could use flashcards to try to translate entire English sentences into French near-verbatim. They may get you to think in French, but they can be immensely stressful. Stress can be a good thing but not so much for the kind that causes you to lose motivation and take extended time off from learning. You'll naturally make faster progress when you enjoy the learning process and do it on a consistent daily basis.

A handful of hardcore French learners out there may determine that they just need to study for three or more hours a day to achieve the results they desire. We understand this deep and burning desire to learn, and we have even previously identified ourselves with that level of hard work. The truth is, however, that you don't have to study for three or more hours each day to achieve fluency. You can get fluent in French with just 45-90 minutes everyday of intensive learning followed by a habit of regularly reading, watching, and listening to material in French. This is considerably easier to maintain in the long-term and can generate greater results because of consistency.

45-90 minutes of intensive learning each day might not seem enough when there are thousands of words to learn. It might seem like we should spend three or more hours studying every day considering all of the phrasebooks, short stories, coursebooks, grammar books, newspaper articles, apps, and online tools available.

If you have ever reached the intermediate stages of a foreign language, you might have experienced some frustration in trying to manage all of this learning. You forget words. You forget grammar rules that you have read multiple times. And of course, native speakers still talk too fast. It's quite easy to find yourself in language learning hell.

The Language Learning Bubble

Many dedicated language learners burnout after trying so hard to learn, but the term "burnout" does not quite capture this problem in full. The real issue preventing many people from learning a foreign language is their definition of what it means to learn languages. That problematic definition is formed from being required to take unimaginative and uninspired Spanish and French classes in high school and college. That definition is what causes burnout.

In the beginner phase or at any level, it would be a huge mistake to exclude content made by native speakers for native speakers in the target language. We aren't talking about *good* and *educational* sources to learn conversational French from. We mean content that is fun and deeply interesting to you. You can learn from the native material that you love like French movies, TV shows, websites, videos, books, and video games. Beginners to language learning often omit this content in favor of more traditional learning from materials like textbooks, online courses, and audio lessons.

It's so easy to become trapped and confined within a bubble of language learning materials. Learning can become stale and boring and come to a dead halt. These breaks can last for days, weeks, or months until the motivation to continue learning returns. Millions of people who start learning a language quit all together before ever reaching fluency. This book aims to prevent that from happening to you.

Many language learners do not allow themselves to freely read, listen, or watch these materials in only the foreign language, and it's easy to understand why. In these instructional materials, everything is broken down and explained so that it is easy to grasp. In native materials, it's the exact opposite. Nothing is broken down nor explained. Your efforts to learn here can feel like trying to drain a lake using only a single cup as a tool. It can feel nearly impossible and highly uncomfortable when you can't understand anything that is going on.

The real French language and the real fun in learning it, however, lies outside the bubble of instructional materials. It can feel like there is a massive set of essential vocabulary that we absolutely must know before tackling these fun materials, and if we do not know them, we feel we aren't ready yet. That feeling, however, is sure to keep us trapped in the language learning bubble. What is absolutely essential is that we enjoy the learning process every single day. If we truly appreciate the learning process day by day, we will eventually learn everything that we wish to know.

But how do you learn from fun things like French movies and TV shows? Do you continually stop to look up each new word that you find? When do you actually just watch, read, and listen? The hardcore learner might try to learn every new word, but that is a surefire way to burn yourself out. And when we just let ourselves watch, read, and listen, it can feel like we aren't learning anything at all.

It's easy to give up trying to learn from the fun things that we truly care about. It's easy to find yourself surrounded by thousands of words and question their usefulness in everyday conversation. Why would we ever need to know "alpha strike" and "aqua prison" from video games when we should be learning practical things like "take out the trash" and "job interview"?

But the truth is that you can learn all of these words and learn them easily. This book will show you how to balance all of this practical French and fantasy French and retain it effectively. You can learn from what you love and use it to learn practical vocabulary and phrases as you go along. Love is what makes all of this learning possible. Without love, learning is meaningless.

So, How Do Polyglots Learn?

Polyglots use a variety of techniques and methods to learn including by not limited to Anki and active recall, context-based learning, high frequency word learning, Shadowing, extensive reading, native materials, immersion, and frequent communication with native speakers. We will explore how you can apply these strategies to create your own self-learning program to master French to fluency and beyond. This includes an approach that we would like to share with you that combines all of these language learning techniques into one. It is by no means the standard approach that all polyglots use, but it is one application of these faster and more effective methods that will allow you to easily learn from almost any native material that you like.

This approach would allow anyone to quickly memorize thousands of vocabulary words, phrases, and grammar points with very little stress involved. It combines both the streamlined learning from language learning materials and the real language from native materials. We enjoy it so much that we felt compelled to write this book to share that method with others who might be looking for more fun and effective ways to learn French and other foreign languages.

Each chapter of this book will cover powerful language learning techniques and gradually expand on the overall main approach this book offers, but for now, here is a brief summary of that approach. Immerse yourself in any kind of French material that you love without any English subtitles or translations for roughly 20 minutes or so. This can include reading up on topics that you are highly interested in, watching exciting French shows and movies, listening to your favorite music, or even playing video games in French.

For this brief amount of time, very carefully listen and look for words unknown to you and that are repeated multiple times. Without stopping the reading, video, or audio, quickly jot down the unknown words that are repeated two or more times and continue without looking anything up in the dictionary. Include the page numbers, video times, audio track times, or in-game screenshots for reference later.

After the 20 minutes or so have passed, stop and review your jotted notes, and pick the two lines or words that you are the most curious to learn. This will be easier to do with written materials, and some effort may be required to find video materials with transcriptions and subtitles in French. Next, use online dictionaries and grammar resources to quickly break down the lines to learn their meaning. After fully learning these lines, create very specific reading, writing, listening, and speaking practice exercises using a free program called Anki (*www.ankisrs.net*). These exercises will help you practice both the lines you select and the more practical example sentences you find in online dictionaries and grammar resources.

As you consistently mine a particular topic, genre, or series and regularly do these exercises, you will come to understand more of it very fast. You'll be actively searching for the high frequency words and learning them. These words are the key to slowly understanding what everyone is saying and what the main idea is. The Anki exercises are just as important in not forgetting those key words. This includes being able to recognize them by eye and ear and produce them when writing or speaking.

If you are in the beginning stages of learning French, this technique is highly recommended as you progress through learning the basics of the language. Reading, breaking down, and learning from native materials like videos, blogs, and novels will be difficult at first, but early attempts to learn from these materials will immediately connect you to the real language used by French native speakers every day. This connection will be sure to bring you excitement. It will also help build an early habit of freely reading, listening to, and watching native French materials without English. A later chapter will cover how to incorporate this method as you learn the basics of French.

The main method of this book aims to keep you highly interested and continually learning until you have reached a level that you are personally satisfied with. When you combine this kind of learning from native materials, learning from traditional language learning materials, creating and doing smart Anki exercises, and frequent interaction with native speakers in your free time, you will have the foundation for an effective learning routine. With this foundation, you are free to choose and mix what native sources and language learning resources you would like to use. We invite you to experiment with these language learning strategies and see what brings you the most benefit and enjoyment in your journey to learn French.

Part I will continue with an explanation about the Anki exercises and how to create them from any French material. Part II will cover how to create your own individualized learning program from the foreign material that you love. We hope you enjoy this book and find it helpful in simplifying the language learning process.

FASTER WAYS TO LEARN

In general, rereading and rewriting new vocabulary, phrases, and sentences in mass is not very efficient in helping you retain that new information. You may also find it tedious and boring. Anki aims to improve your memory of new information by testing your ability to actively recall it through intelligent flashcard exercises.

We don't like to say the method of this book is flashcards because we were all taught to use boring, primitive flashcards in our school days. We speak of the ones where the front side would read "this animal has eyes bigger than its brain" and the back would read "ostrich." They were dry and dull, and they remind us of the useless facts that we were required to memorize for school tests and forgot just a week later.

In this book, we will look at Production, Cloze, Listening, and Shadowing exercises. Two rules govern these exercises. First, choose easy. Second, choose fun.

These rules act as daily reminders to prevent the burnout that causes many language learners to quit temporarily or indefinitely. These four exercise types will help you to fully understand any new vocabulary, phrases, and grammar that you wish to learn and master. They will train you in all five of the language skills: reading, writing, speaking, listening, and thinking.

This chapter is dedicated to describing the purpose of each exercise, and the rationale behind why specifically these exercises were chosen. A set of examples, images, and how to instructions will be provided in the next chapter.

Production

Let us begin with the basic flashcard exercise that you are probably already familiar with. You might have made a few of these if you have ever used flashcards or Anki to help you learn a foreign language. Simply, you'll be given a word in English or a picture and have to say aloud the equivalent word in French. That's it.

We imagine that some language learners out there hold a strong dislike for this kind of exercise, and we can understand why. It can get really boring really fast. These exercises alone are unable to hold our attention for very long, but that's the thing. It's just one of many tools and one with a very important use. The problem arises when you do nothing but this exercise in Anki.

When you have a strong mix and balance of other exercises to go with this simple one, this exercise is perfect. Our ability to speak a new language is greatly enhanced just by being able to recall thousands of vocabulary and phrases with lightning speed and little to no trouble. We need to know how to quickly say things like "bleu" (blue), "cercle" (circle), "conducteur de bus" (bus driver), "carton de lait" (milk carton), "avoir mal à la gorge" (to have a sore throat), "faire la vaisselle" (to wash the dishes), "Allumer les lumières" (to turn on the lights), and "brancher" (to plug in). That's where Production exercises in the right quantity can help us.

What if we reverse the order and put French on the front and English on the back? This would change the Production exercise to a reading and translation exercise, which is useful, yet we will get plenty of reading from the Cloze and Shadowing exercises. Additionally, the Listening exercises will give us a more interesting way to test our recognition of these words.

Putting just the English word on the front side of this flashcard saves a lot of time, and you could also put an image representing the word here in an effort to use as little English as possible. The choice is yours. Abstract words like "distraction" (distraction) and "recharge" (refill) will be much more difficult to find proper images for, so the English word might be the easiest option. If you are looking to learn with as little as English as possible in Anki, Cloze exercises offer an alternative way to test our recall ability for these abstract words.

Stick with just single words and small phrases. If we put lengthy English sentences on the front and try to recall them in full in the target language as briefly mentioned last chapter, we can potentially put ourselves through language learning hell. The possibility of all kinds of synonyms and different translations makes it frustrating. Too many questions come up when we think of answers in our minds that seem correct yet are different from the answer on the back. You might find yourself irritated wondering whether or not the answer that you came up with is correct or not. It's tedious and not a very pleasant learning experience.

Let's say we want to learn from a basic sentence like "Lorsque tu arrives à Paris, appelle-moi" which means "When you are in Paris, call me". Instead of trying to memorize the full sentence, use these basic Production exercises to help you memorize single words like "arriver" (to arrive) and "appeler" (to call). Make exercises for very short phrases like "appelle-moi" (call me [informal]) and "lorsque tu arrives" (when you arrive [informal]).

In these Production exercises, we can test not only our ability to recall vocabulary and phrases but to say these words with correct pronunciation and phonetic stress. Take this time to work on reducing your accent as you say aloud new words that you are learning. Pay special attention to properly producing each sound like a native speaker would. This special attention makes all the difference between a thick and goofy accent and an authentic French accent. For example, when you see "to arrive" on the front side of this flashcard exercise, instead of just quickly muttering "arriver", say it aloud and really focus on the guttural [ʁ] sound here (voiced uvular fricative) to make it sound native.

To truly speak French with proper pronunciation, there are a large number of phonetic issues that you face as a non-native speaker. You will need to train yourself to produce this [ʁ] sound found in "arriver" but also other sounds like the vowels [y] (close front rounded vowel) and [ø] (close-mid front rounded vowel). They are not found in modern day English, but they can be learned by anyone. Production exercises can help you to make these sounds come automatically to your tongue through repetition while also challenging your mind to recall all kinds of vocabulary. Use these exercises to practice and correct these phonetic issues. French phonetics will be discussed much more in detail in Chapter four.

Cloze

On the front side of these cards, we will be presented with a small context (a sentence or a few sentences) that we have learned fully beforehand except that one small piece will be missing. The objective is to figure out what is missing based on the surrounding context and write the answer in our notebook. That missing piece will be a single word which can be a vocabulary word or a piece of grammar. This simple exercise will require us to think in French while strengthening our reading and writing skills and building our vocabulary and grammar knowledge with virtually no stress.

Context makes these challenges interesting and fun. Test for the right vocabulary in context. Test and learn new phrases one word at a time. Test for those tricky French verb conjugations in context (present, imperfect, conditional, future, subjunctive). Test for the correct grammar particle which can seem so oddly specific at times. This includes gendered nouns and pronouns in French (le, la, les, l', un, une, il, ils, elle, elles). To summarize, if something is new or still unfamiliar to you in a sentence, make a Cloze card.

There is no need to write any word more than once. There is no need to test for large amounts of missing information. There is no need to copy whole sentences down in our notebook. There is no need to memorize these sentences to recite later. Instead, we will see all of the new vocabulary, phrases, and grammar points again and again in the variety of Anki cards that we will make for each context that we choose from our coursebooks and native materials. And while we are testing ourselves on something small, we will still need to use the other information to help us determine the missing piece.

Of course we can use Production exercises to test the gender of nouns (le, la) as well as verb conjugations, yet Cloze exercises offer an additional means to strengthen vocabulary and grammar with the power of context. They get us to actively read and write the language. They are helpful for language pattern recognition, sentence building, and even spelling. It builds up reading comprehension like no other. In the intermediate and advanced learning stages, even long and challenging passages can be broken up, practiced, and conquered one word at a time.

Reading, thinking, and writing in the target language are all involved. Many of us dream to be able to think in foreign languages, so here is a start. Here we are reading and thinking in the foreign language while actively trying to find the one missing word. We then write the answer in that language in our notebooks. It's just one word written one time.

It may look like a silly and simple elementary school exercise, but it's a highly effective strategy to help you learn any difficult piece of language one word at a time. Remove just "lorsque" or "quand" from sentences and practice figuring out which one should be used. The same goes for "connaître" vs "savoir" and other confusing language structures. Learn new expressions like "Faire la grasse matinée" (to sleep in) one word at a time. Make cards for even the easy vocabulary you are very familiar with that are found within these new structures and phrases. It's an easy way to memorize longer phrases.

It's strongly recommended to test only one word at a time. Imagine that we wanted to learn a new expression or phrase composed of a group of words, and we created a single Cloze card where we needed to write this group of words. When several words are missing, there is much less context to work with. When even two or three words are missing from a sentence, there might not be enough context to be able to figure out what exactly is missing. And we would have to remember the exact group of words missing in the sentence from all the possible synonyms. To avoid this frustration, test only word at a time.

Listening

The Listening exercises are simply listening more or less, but text-to-speech programs can completely change how we practice foreign listening comprehension these days. There exists a way to take words, phrases, and sentences from any source at all and generate free audio recordings of an automated native speaker saying those words. These audio recordings can then be placed inside of Anki to make listening the easiest and most fun language skill to practice. Amazing nor astounding does not even begin to describe this awesome power now available to everybody.

After hearing a two to three second audio file played on the front of these flashcard exercises, it is our task to either think or say aloud the equivalent in our native tongue. We can test our comprehension of single words or sentences in full here. After the file is played, it's either we get it or don't within the next three seconds. It's a very simple and effective exercise in training our valuable ears to instantly decode meaning of spoken words just like we can in our first language. The Cloze exercises do take a little time and effort to figure out, but the Listening and Production cards help break up the monotony with on the spot lightning round challenges.

On the back side of these flashcard exercises, we recommend putting the English translation and the French transcription of the audio file to check for complete comprehension. Cloze and potentially Production can be done in only French, but using English here is perhaps the simplest way to check if we fully understand the meaning behind the words. Freely listening to and reading native French material without English will be encouraged throughout this book, yet this will be one of the rare cases where it may be more effective to use our native language.

Unlike the Production cards, however, we can test our comprehension of sentences in full one by one. Undoubtedly, there are going to be some synonyms when translating full sentences from one language to another, but it takes much less effort to translate sentences from the target language to our native language. Try it yourself and see how fast they go by.

Shadowing

This technique is one way to put more French on our tongues. It was developed and popularized by professor Alexander Arguelles, and in its original form, it requires long dialogues and short stories as well as adequate space to march back and forth in. We would like to include a somewhat condensed form of Shadowing that can be done inside of Anki.

There are three types of Shadowing that can be done: Shadowing with no text (Blind Shadowing), Shadowing with the English translation, and Shadowing with the transcription in the foreign language. All of them will include audio in the target language. To set up these exercises, just place the text and audio on the front side and leave the back side blank. Create one card for each type of Shadowing exercise. When these exercises appear during Anki practice sessions, the sound file will automatically play by default, but when you are ready to start, you can replay the sound file by pressing the 'R' button on your keyboard.

Shadowing is as simple as repeating aloud what you are hearing as you hear it to the best of your ability. In Shadowing, you do not repeat after the audio file after it has stopped, but instead, you talk on top of it continuously for the entire recording. Two or three attempts each time will be good enough. If you found the Shadowing difficult, you can tell Anki to retest you again in a few short days so that you can practice it more frequently.

When no text is present, you are focusing solely on the sounds of the language and reproducing them with your mouth. Even though you may have little to no idea what you are saying, the point is to listen intensively and get used to the feeling of speaking foreign sounds. When Shadowing with the English translation, you are still repeating what you hear but now with complete understanding. Don't worry about the exact meaning of each word and how they are phrased but instead just focus on the overall meaning here. And when Shadowing with the French transcription, you are listening, speaking, and reading in French all at once. Use the text to help you pronounce all the words while still focusing on copying the native speaker's intonation and rhythm.

Shadowing is quite the workout at first, and it remains a good method to build our mouth muscles as we encounter more language to mimic. If you are interested in things like intonation, pronunciation, speaking confidence, and accent reduction, this is the technique for you. It's also challenging and incredibly fun.

Unfortunately, this exercise can only be done with video and audio French sources, so written materials will be left out. There are methods to get native French speakers to record such lines, but they are highly inconvenient and are generally not worth the time and money to acquire. Text-to-speech robots are not accurate enough yet to imitate proper intonation, so we do not recommend Shadowing after them.

We will admit that this last exercise requires a few hoops to jump through to setup inside of Anki. We understand that you may not be willing to acquire source files and extract audio from them. If it is too much of a hassle, you can practice Shadowing without Anki.

SPACED RECALL SYSTEM

A nki will allow us to create all of these flashcard exercises, and it also doubles as a Spaced Repetition System (SRS). The SRS aims to test us on information at intervals just before we are likely to forget. This means easy exercises can be pushed back months and months away until the next time we are tested on them. Difficult exercises will be shown more frequently until we master them. If exercises are too difficult, we can change them to make them winnable again.

We have absolute freedom over what we want to focus on and practice, but this freedom comes at a price. We will have to make our own personal decks based on the materials that we use and what we personally need. We must also stick to a schedule of regularly doing these exercises at a certain point in the day but more on this in the final chapter.

We will see the same sentences frequently during our first few Anki sessions, but soon a large variety of hundreds of sentences will take form. Within a few weeks, we will amass a diverse bank of sentences to practice from, and we will rarely see the same context more than once or twice in a session. Seeing this massive range of words and sentences through the four Anki exercises will do many things for us:

1. Allow us to visit a variety of topics in rapid succession.

2. Test our ability to recall words through reading, writing, speaking, and listening.

3. Keep us on our toes with the uncertainty of what is to come next.

4. Enable learning to flow like a fast-paced game.

How to Setup

When you download, install, and open up Anki, click 'Create Deck' and name it whatever you like. We will only need one deck for now, as all four of our flashcards will go into this deck. Click 'Add' at the top, and then 'Basic' at the top of the new window. By default, you should see four card types.

THE ORIGINAL FOUR CARD TYPES IN ANKI

Let's add Production, Listening, and Shadowing cards. Creating card types for each one takes seconds and allows for easy reference and organization if we ever wish to change something in bulk. If you click "Manage", you can delete the unnecessary cards and keep "Cloze". Click "Add" and select "Add:Basic" and rename it to "Production". Repeat this process for "Listening" and "Shadowing."

Next, you will need an add-on called "AwesomeTTS" (*https://ankiweb.net/shared/info/301952613*). It offers multiple free Text to Speech services that we can integrate into Anki. This will allow us to do the Listening card types as well as add an extra audio reinforcement to our Production and Cloze cards. With a simple install and Anki reboot, we can simply paste the word or sentence into the 'Front' or 'Back' box, highlight it, and click the speaker icon from the add-on to quickly generate the audio in seconds. In case AwesomeTTS is ever removed for any reason, the internet provides multiple free Text to Speech services that can be used as a replacement. Let us take this time to be grateful for this technology and how it makes life a little bit easier.

Remember to switch card types when creating exercises. To switch card types, if we are looking at a new blank card, click "Type" and select the appropriate exercise.

Inserting Images and Audio

Images and audio from language learning and native materials aren't required, but they are a means to create a stronger link from what we are learning inside Anki to what we are reading and listening to every day. Images and the original audio files can make Anki all the more real, and your efforts here will be rewarded.

Images and audio from videos can be useful in Production, Cloze, and Shadowing cards to add context. Images are super easy to insert. Press the 'PrtSc' button (Command + Shift + 3 for Macs) on your keyboard while the video is on the screen and paused at the appropriate moment. Then, we will need to open up a basic image editing program like Paint in Windows (Paintbrush for Macs) and crop the image to our liking before saving it. When adding cards to Anki, make sure the cursor is in the 'Front' text box, and click the paperclip icon to add our image.

Coursebooks and textbooks provide easy access to native speaker recordings via CD, but inserting audio from native-level materials is a little more difficult. For educational purposes, you will need to obtain the original audio or video source. There are of course many ways to create the audio clip we want, but we found the free audio editing program Audacity (*http://www.audacityteam.org*) to work well enough.

In order to import video files into Audacity, however, we will need to install the FFmpeg library file. This add-on is supported by the Audacity developers and is provided on their website. It can also be found with a simple internet search with the words "FFmpeg library audacity."

<u>FFmpeg Library for Audacity:</u>

<u>http://manual.audacityteam.org/man/faq_installation_and _plug_ins.html#How_do_I_download_and_install_the_F Fmpeg_Import.2FExport_Library.3F</u>

After opening the file with Audacity, we can use the times in the original audio or video file to find our selected passage with ease. Use the mouse to highlight the clip needed, press the stop button, and go to 'File' and then 'Export Selected Audio...' to create the audio clip needed. We can use the paperclip icon in Anki to insert these audio clips just as we did with the images.

Here's an example of extracting audio from a video:

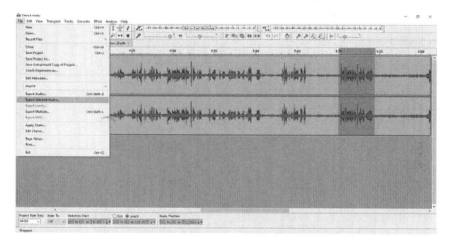

EXTRACTING AUDIO FROM VIDEO WITH AUDACITY

The images help to add more context. The original image and audio can make Anki sessions much more meaningful and memorable:

A SHADOWING EXERCISE COMPLETE WITH AN IMAGE AND AUDIO

Example Passage

To demonstrate these exercises in action, we will use a scene from the first few minutes of the movie *Un peu, beaucoup, aveuglément!*. Let's break it down and see what exercises we can create to master any potentially new language in this scene.

Sample Context:

Alors, je suis venu vous distraire
et peut-être vous faire rire.
Un sourire?

Translation:

So, I came (here) to amuse you
and maybe even make you laugh.
Hey, a smile?

Quick Breakdown:

alors --- so (conjunction)

je suis --- I am

venu --- came (past form of venir)

vous --- you [formal]

distraire --- to amuse / entertain / distract

et --- and

peut-être --- maybe

faire --- to make / do

rire --- to laugh

un sourire --- a smile

Anki Practice Exercises:

Here's just one out of many possible combinations of Anki exercises that you could make for these sentences:

to amuse / entertain / distract

Production # 1: distraire

maybe

Production # 2: peut-être

I have come to...

Production # 3: Je suis venu...

to laugh

Production # 4: rire

to make someone laugh

Production# 5: *faire rire*

Alors, je suis [...] vous distraire et peut-être vous faire rire.

Un sourire?

Cloze # 1: venu

Alors, je suis venu vous   [...]

et peut-être vous faire rire.

Un sourire?

Cloze # 2: distraire

Alors, je suis venu vous distraire

et peut-être vous [...] rire.

Un sourire?

Cloze # 3: faire

Alors, je suis venu vous distraire

et peut-être vous faire [...] .

Un sourire?

Cloze # 4: rire

distraire

(audio file)

Listening # 1: to amuse / entertain / distract

peut-être

(audio file)

Listening # 2: maybe

Je suis venu

(audio file)

Listening # 3: I have come to...

rire

(audio file)

Listening # 4: to laugh

faire rire

(audio file)

Listening # 5: to make someone laugh

Shadowing # 1: with no text

So, I came (here) to amuse you

and maybe even make you laugh.

Hey, a smile?

Shadowing # 2: with English translation

Alors, je suis venu vous distraire

et peut-être vous faire rire.

Un sourire?

Shadowing # 3: with French transcription

A high amount of Production and Listening, a moderate amount of Cloze, and a low amount of Shadowing has worked well for us in the past, but feel free to experiment with the ratio. You can also experiment with different sources to create exercises with as you will see in the second half to this book.

PART TWO

Moving Towards Immersion

STARTING FROM ZERO

E arly attempts to learn from native French materials like movies are most definitely encouraged for beginners, but without learning the basics of French as you progress, your language ability will be very limited. You're likely to have some trouble getting around French speaking countries if you don't know basic French phrases or how to construct basic sentences. Without knowing the differences between polite speech and casual speech, you could come off as a little arrogant to native French speakers. And speaking without proper pronunciation can make it very difficult for native speakers to understand you.

This chapter will be a collection of advice and strategies that you may find useful if you are a beginner or are currently working your way through a French language course or book at any level. There are so many ways to begin learning a foreign language these days, and we don't wish to dictate an exact process of how beginners should get started. That should be your choice. Start wherever you are drawn to the most!

You will have more success the more you focus on the things that truly interest you. A few people will study only phonetics at first for months and perhaps even a full year or two with the goal of sounding as native-like as possible. Some will dive straight in and try communicating with French native speakers on day one. Others may be looking for a more guided approach, so they use websites and apps like Duolingo. Start with whatever excites you the most.

In the age of technology, quick internet searches, and YouTube, it is possible to learn anything including a foreign language without classroom instruction or even a single textbook. For the sake of streamlined learning, however, we would recommend a coursebook or textbook but a maximum of just one. A high-quality coursebook does provide well-rounded introductions to foreign languages, solid grammar explanations, and a wealth of words, phrases, and sentences to create Anki exercises with.

Coursebooks and other French learning resources provide a safe and sheltered source for learning, yet it is important to escape this language learning bubble as early as possible. Outside of that is where the true language and culture lie. There may be a set of six textbooks to learn French, but you may only need the first one before you are able to learn primarily from material made for native speakers. Smart Anki use and a habit of immersing yourself in native materials frequently can make that happen easily.

French Pronunciation

Regardless of whatever material you choose to begin learning with, incorporating phonetics early on in your program is highly recommended. Learning to speak with correct pronunciation should be a part of every program to master the French language or any other language. French phonetic knowledge and training will make your speech much easier for native speakers to understand. They will notice the hard work you put into not just being able to communicate with them but also sounding similar to them. That is sure to make conversations much more comfortable and pleasant.

When practicing pronunciation or when learning new vocabulary, repeating words after a native speaker and attempting to mimic them is generally good practice, but without phonetic knowledge or training, you are likely to still speak with a rather thick accent. When we learn to speak new languages, we unconsciously and unknowingly project and apply the phonetic rules from our first language. We are hardwired to the speech patterns of our native language after speaking it for so long. As a result, there are sounds in French that you might not be able to recognize by ear and thus be unable to mimic without some basic phonetic training. The good news is that this knowledge and training is easy to obtain and master with a little time and effort.

It's as easy as studying the sounds of French vowels and consonants and consistent practice. Some French learners decide to skip this step without realizing its true importance, and the consequences of this decision can be found in their speech. You can tell who took the time to practice and master the basic vowel sounds like [y], [œ], and [ø] and who did not. They may be completely new sounds to you if you are a native English speaker, so they need to be heard and practiced with persistence if you are going to be able to produce them on command. And Production and Shadowing exercises offer such training methods.

The International Phonetic Alphabet (IPA) symbols may also be new to you if you have never studied phonetics before. It can be a little overwhelming when looking at the entire IPA system, yet there is no need to study each individual letter and diacritic. You will only need to learn the symbols for the new sounds in French and a few in English that will help you to make these new sounds. These symbols and their sounds will become familiar to you in just a few short days or weeks of practice.

To produce the [y] sound like in "tu" (you), start with the [i] vowel sound (the "ee" in "see") which you already know how to produce. Make that sound aloud and hold it for a few seconds. While producing this sound, round your lips like you would when you make the "wh" sound (like in "who") without moving your tongue at all. Your tongue will naturally want to move backwards, but if you keep it still, you will make the [y] sound.

To do the [œ] sound like in "œuf" (egg), first make the [ɛ] sound (the "e" in "bed"). Now, round your lips. That creates the [œ] sound. And to make the [ø] sound like in "deux" (two), we will need the [e] sound found in "play". At the end of the word "play", you can hear [eɪ], which is two vowel sounds (also known as a diphthong). Make and hold the [e] sound and then round your lips. That makes the [ø] sound.

There are other somewhat new vowel sounds in French, which are closer to their English counterparts, but these can be learned easily through simple mimicry. It is the three rounded vowels [y], [œ], and [ø] that will require the most attention if you are native speaker of English. If practiced on a daily basis in the context of new vocabulary, however, these vowels and all French vowels will come to you naturally as the English ones do.

Looking at the new consonants in French, there are [ɲ], [ɥ], and [ʁ]. To make the [ɲ] found in words like "agneau" (lamb), simply put the middle of your tongue on the roof of your mouth. It sounds like you're trying to say "nyah". The [ɥ] sound in words like "huit" (eight) can be made by first starting with the English word "shoe". Say the word aloud and hold the last vowel sound which will be [u]. From this [u], switch to the [i] sound (the "ee" in "see") quickly. This rapid sliding of the tongue makes the [ɥ] sound.

The infamous French guttural "R" [ʁ] is a common complaint amongst native English speakers learning French and other European languages, but such complaints will bring you no closer to perfect pronunciation. They are a waste of your time and energy. Resolve to conquer the French "R" today.

There are four common variations that are used, and you'll hear them all when you listen to native French speakers. They are the uvular trill [ʀ], the voiced uvular fricative [ʁ], the uvular approximant [ʁ], and the voiceless uvular fricative [χ]. Which ones are used varies from person to person, but they are all made with the uvula and back of the tongue. And they all make a gargling sound as if you were trying to spit something up. We recommend using the voiced uvular fricative [ʁ], as it is the most common in France.

It's also highly recommended to listen to the differences between these four sounds to gather a more complete understanding that our written explanation cannot provide. Perhaps one of the best demonstrations of these guttural sounds online can be found at *https://www.youtube.com/watch? v=hI2Pso1dDjM*. This video can also be found by searching YouTube for "French Pronunciation: The Sounds of French (aka "How to learn lots of new vowels"). As an added bonus, this video also provides demonstrations for the other sounds discussed in this chapter.

Let's quickly go through some other pronunciation mistakes that non-native French speakers may not pick up on. The French "P", "T", and "K" letters are shorter than they are in English. Instead of saying "pah", "tah", and "kah", drop the "ah" and keep them short. The French "L" uses only the tip of the tongue and much less tongue comparatively to the English "L". Try saying "la" but using only the tip of your tongue. These small adjustments should be much easier compared to all the other sounds that we have covered.

There are many silent letters in French, and more often than not the last letter at the end of a word is silent. And in fact, every "H" in French is silent. But there are muted "H"s like in "herbe" (grass) and aspirated "H"s in words like "hallion" (rag). Muted "H"s contract to make "l'herbe" (the grass), but aspirated "H"s do not like in "le haillon" (the rag). And finally, unlike English, contractions in

French are mandatory. "Le homme" is incorrect. You must use "l'homme".

That's Too Many Rules!

All of these pronunciation rules can be quite overwhelming, but there's no need to memorize all of the rules like you would cram for a school test. Practice them as you learn vocabulary. Carefully listen to how native speakers pronounce these words. Refer back to the rules whenever you are confused about anything.

It is highly recommended that you listen to an audio recording of each new word that you learn. These recordings can be easily found in online dictionaries like Collins Dictionary (*https://www.collinsdictionary.com/us/dictionary/english-french*). Carefully check the IPA pronunciation key and listen for these new sounds and patterns. And then, simply copy and practice them. The more words that you learn how to say correctly the easier pronunciation becomes.

Now that you are more aware of these sounds, you'll slowly begin to notice them when listening to native speakers. You will be able to properly mimic these sounds and gradually incorporate them into your spoken French. When doing the Production and Shadowing exercises, that's when you can really begin to build a natural intuition for how to pronounce words and speak with proper intonation. On the back of Production cards, you can even include a text-to-speech recording of each word and short phrase for a quick pronunciation reference.

If you are not a beginner but were unaware of some of these phonetic rules, there is no need to worry. This new phonetic awareness will slowly shape your pronunciation over time when paired with consistent pronunciation practice like the Production and Shadowing exercises. You can always rewrite any bad speaking habits that you may have developed thus far. Some learners even go as far as to record themselves to compare with a native speaker or to check on their progress from time to time.

French Dialects

Of course, pronunciation and also a considerable amount of vocabulary change depending on which country you go to. At the time of writing this book, French is the official language in 29 different countries, but Parisian French is considered the standard. It is what most French learning materials will teach you. Even within the country of France, however, you will find several dialects such as the southern Marseille and Toulouse varieties. French people understand the full range of dialects within their country, and so can you in time.

Start with the standard Parisian French and branch outward as you read and listen to native materials from French speakers from all across the world. You'll find a common European French spoken in countries like Belgium, Switzerland, and Luxembourg with minor differences in dialects and region-specific vocabulary.

It is when you step outside of Europe that you will find find a massive variety of dialects and region-specific vocabularies depending on which of the other French-speaking countries you visit. While Haiti does list their official language as French, the French-based creole language called Haitian Creole is what you will hear spoken on the street. In Africa, there is no single, unified African French language. West and Central, East, Maghreb, and Djibouti speak different dialects of French alongside Arabic and other local indigenous languages which results in a tremendous variety of vocabulary and expressions.

Québécois (Quebec French) and Canadian French have very notable differences than the French spoken in Europe and elsewhere. They have been more heavily influenced by Great Britain and the United States, and as a result, they have adopted many more English words into their colloquial vocabulary. Many of its words, idioms, and cultural references may confuse French speakers from elsewhere. On the other hand, The formal language is much more aligned with European French and can be mostly understood by francophones.

If you have a specific country that you plan on traveling to or a specific nationality of people in mind that you want to communicate with, it would be most wise to learn its region-specific vocabulary and dialect as you progress in learning standardized French. For example, if you wish to learn Quebec French, there are plenty of resources and native speakers available to specifically teach that dialect.

Rather than overwhelming you with a long list of regional variations of French words, we want to focus on giving you the means to conquer whatever vocabulary and whichever countries that you wish to take on. As an example, you might first learn that a "taille-crayon" means pencil sharpener and later encounter "aiguisoir" in Canada which is used to mean the same thing. To remember this difference, we can make additional Anki cards asking us to recall pencil sharpener in different countries. In the case of these stand-alone words, simply make a Production card for "pencil sharpener (Quebec)" and a Listening card for "aiguisoir" (pencil sharpener (Quebec))".

These regional differences are not so much different than English. If you grow up in an English speaking country, you can travel to any other English speaking country in the world and still be able to communicate with almost anyone. You may need to learn a few new words to prevent any future confusion or misunderstandings, but everyone will be able to understand you regardless of your dialect.

Working Towards Immersion

After this introduction to the basic sounds of French, there will be four learning activities that require a bit of balancing: learning from your coursebook or primary course, Anki practice, learning directly from native French materials, and communicating with native speakers in French. Cycle between multiple activities every day and try not to get caught up in focusing on just one. They are equally important. This cycle and variety in your daily routine will be sure to maximize your attention span and help you absorb even more new vocabulary.

If you are unsure about how much time you can commit to learning French daily, start with doing just one of these activities for 30-60 minutes each day. If you manage your time well and work fast enough, you might even be able to squeeze in two smaller learning activities during this small period of time. The more learning activities the better. Creating and maintaining this daily habit of language learning will be one of your first challenges.

Doing French three times a week will not cut it. Languages are not just knowledge but also a set of skills our eyes, ears, mouths, hands, and heads must practice daily in order to achieve fluency. If you can only make the time to watch 20 minutes of video content with no subtitles for the day, so be it. You may not learn much for that day, but these small yet consistent actions do build towards new habits that will enable you to make this major lifestyle change.

Focus on not breaking the daily language learning habit at all costs. Consistency builds habits. Once that consistency and priority in learning French has been established, you can slowly build upon this routine by incorporating more activities.

It's highly recommended to try to communicate with native speakers in French very early on in the language learning process. Some polyglots go as far as to speak with tutors from day one in only the target language. This early conversation will be quite limited of course, yet it will train you to be fearless in your efforts to communicate regardless of your current level. Use online dictionaries to look up words as much you need to. It will train you to be accustomed to and comfortable with making mistakes, receiving corrections, and learning from them. In the last chapter, we will discuss ways to get into contact with native speakers and get corrections.

While accumulating more and more vocabulary and grammar from a variety of materials, it's important to build up your ability to communicate your thoughts fluently through writing and speaking. If you want fluency, it would be most wise to write or speak French every single day. For some folks, adding this additional activity to an already hour-long language learning routine might be really hard to follow every day. If you are having trouble staying consistent with this commitment, aim first for an absolute minimum of 30-60 minutes every day.

Whenever you're ready, try two or even three of these learning activities each day. If you can manage such a routine consistently, you will be sure to learn at an accelerated rate. If your goal is fluency, consider making one of these activities an output (writing or speaking) activity. Make writing or speaking a permanent part of your daily routine to ensure your ability to communicate well with native speakers.

Doing four or more intensive learning activities every day is not recommended. When strict study time begins to exceed two or even three hours, you'll begin to run into problems similar to those mentioned in the first chapter. If you would like to learn even more after these intensive learning activities are completed, try adding in extensive activities to do in your free time. In comparison, these are much more relaxed and laid back.

Think of these extensive activities as French hobbies. This includes watching exciting TV shows without subtitles, reading in French on topics that you are highly interested in, and making friends with native speakers. Do the things that truly interest you and stir excitement from deep within. Unlike the method described in the first chapter, here we aren't trying to learn anything at all. Take this time to get to know French-speaking people and enjoy French material for the subject matter alone! Higher reading, listening, speaking, and writing skills will come as a natural result of spending hundreds and thousands of hours living through the language.

The secret to being consistent in these extensive activities lies in finding the French hobbies that you truly care about. For example, if what you love to do is play video games in your free time, change the language settings to French and don't look back. In fact, it may help to envision yourself as someone from France or another French-speaking country. It may sound silly, but this kind of creative thinking will enable you to replace your old English hobbies one by one permanently.

If you wish to learn full-time or go full immersion in your home environment, it is highly recommended to cycle between multiple extensive activities each day in time-boxed sessions of 20-45 minutes for each activity. You can also take 20-45 minutes at a time to replace more and more of your life with the French language. Some of these steps towards immersion we can immediately get used to, but others may take years in order to overwrite old habits that are strongly rooted in our native language.

Here are some ideas. Delete all songs in English from your music library and replace it with music in French. Change your computer and phone's language. Delete all non-essential English internet bookmarks and replace them with fun French websites.

How to Master Your Textbook

Your textbook should be your loyal and faithful servant and not the other way around. Do not let it become your master. What we mean is that it should not take up the majority of your study and learning time.

Let these books briefly serve you, and then, dismiss them. Seek 5-10 minute explanations for new language and grammar structures. Don't bother with drills and grammatical exercises if they don't interest you. Don't write words out over and over. Don't bore yourself with the comprehension questions in the book. Understand the gist and get out of there! The four super flashcard exercises will make sure that we receive more than enough practice. Use your coursebook time to feed Anki the new information that you wish to practice.

Here are some general rules that may help clear some confusion on what exercises to make as you progress through your book. For new vocabulary words and set phrases, create one Production and one Listening card. For every major grammar point or topic covered, grab three, four, or five sentences and make one Listening card for each. It's not necessary to turn every new sentence into an Anki card, or otherwise, you might fall asleep before you make it to the next chapter!

In these three, four, or five example sentences, use Cloze cards to test for correct grammar usage, but testing for specific vocabulary in these sentences may not be the best idea. Cloze cards testing for specific vocabulary and phrases tend to work better for dialogues and other larger contexts rather than these stand-alone example sentences. Short example sentences often do not provide enough context to make the answer clear and unambiguous. If there is a specific vocabulary word or phrase that we wish to practice, multiple correct answers can interfere. Stick with larger and more memorable contexts to test vocabulary and phrases with Cloze cards.

Monologues, dialogues, and long passages found in textbooks are perfect for Cloze as well as Shadowing exercises. These scenarios provide good opportunities to speak alongside a native speaker and to try to keep up with their intonation and speed to the best of our ability. Use Production, Cloze, and Listening as you see fit to breakdown all the new vocabulary, phrases, and grammar in these larger contexts. The Shadowing cards may be few and far in between in practice sessions, but you can use these gigantic gaps to gauge your personal progress as you eventually encounter each one.

French Verbs

Verb conjugation tables can be tackled with Production and Listening exercises. French verb conjugations can be very overwhelming when presented with all the possible conjugations of even a single verb. There is no need, however, to make Anki cards for every possible conjugation. That wouldn't be easy or fun. Instead, master the verb tenses one by one.

If you are an absolute beginner, start with the present tense conjugations for "-er", "-ir", and "-re" verbs. We recommend starting with one verb for each like "parler" (to speak), "finir" (to finish), and "entendre" (to hear). Make Production and Listening cards for "je", "tu", "il/elle/on", "nous", "vous", and "ils/elles".

Rather than make one Production and one Listening for every form, split the conjugations however you wish between the two exercises to save time. For example, make Production cards for "I speak" (parle), "he/she/people speak" (parle), and "you (all) speak" (parlez). Make Listening cards for "parles" (you speak [informal]), "parlons" (we speak), "parlent" (they speak).

For those unaware, "vous" is the polite word for you. The "vous" conjugation (parlez) should be used when talking with people you do not know well, people older than yourself, or people in a higher position of power than yourself. "Tu" and its conjugation (parles) are informal and should be only used with people you know very well, people who are the same age as you or younger, or those in a similar social standing as yourself. "Tú" can be used with family, friends, peers, and children.

"On" and its conjugation (parle) are a bit more complicated. "On" literally means "one" like in "one speaks", but it is very commonly used in spoken French to mean "we", "people", "you", "someone", "they", and even "I". Determining the exact meaning of the pronoun is a matter of context. It's a way of speaking that is best understood through hours and hours of practice. In fact, "on" is used much more commonly than "nous" to say "we" in colloquial French. In modern French, "nous" and its conjugation can be used to emphasize "we", but it's most often used only in formal situations.

Next, focus on the most common irregular verbs in the present tense like "aller" (to go), "avoir" (to have), "dire" (to say), "voir" (to see), and "être" (to be). Of course, there are many more, but it's important to space them out over several days or even a few weeks rather than to try to tackle 10-20 verbs in a single session each time you learn a new verb tense. Otherwise, that would be way too many cards to create and suck all of the fun out of learning! Do what you can so that you can quickly move on to new topics and have time to read or listen to native French materials and do a little output practice. Refer back to these declension tables if needed when you encounter new conjugations.

Whenever you are ready or whenever it surfaces in your language learning material, begin learning the perfect tense (passé composé). Make Production and Listening cards for 10 or so verbs over several days and pace yourself. Repeat with imperfect, future, conditional, and other tenses one by one as you encounter them. You can always make more of any tense that you wish to practice as you learn new verbs. Looking at our example last chapter, if "distraire" was new or still somewhat unfamiliar to you, consider making exercises for conjugations like "j'ai distrait" (I distracted), "ils distrairont" (they will distract), and "tu aurais distrait" (you would have distracted [informal]).

Remember that all of these exercises should go in one deck to maximize variety during sessions and keep you on your toes. You will never know what is coming up next. Cloze cards will boost our reading skills and our ability to use proper grammar. Production and Listening cards will provide those quick lightning round challenges to boost our recall speed, pronunciation, and listening comprehension. Shadowing cards will challenge us to keep up with the native speaker while also working on our pronunciation and intonation.

A Most Common Mistake

Here's where beginning language learners make the most common mistake. It's a mistake that often puts an early end to many hopeful newcomers in learning a new language. There is no need to finish your initial course or coursebook before you try learning directly from fun native materials. You don't even need to finish the book or course at all! Learn what you can from it until you get bored.

Boredom is our brain's way of telling us that we are going to burn out if we continue to push ourselves to learn from the same material day after day. Our brains are smart that way. It knows when something is no longer working. Resistance to learning doesn't mean that we are stupid or lazy. It means to stop and do something different.

It's so easy to blame ourselves for getting bored because we might feel that we should learn all this serious material before we get to learn from fun materials. That line of thinking, however, is not true at all. Learning from fun materials is the key to never getting bored and quitting.

Hop around materials as you personally see fit! Jump between your coursebook and your true interests in the French language. Whatever you truly desire to learn from is where you should go next. Listening to and following that desire is what keeps you learning. That's the secret to wanting to learn and improve each and every day.

Try to learn directly from native materials as soon as possible. When you personally make the connection between what you are learning from French learning materials to what you see in native materials, that will boost your motivation more than almost anything else. That is how you can eventually conquer all the serious French you feel that you should learn.

Reviewing vs. Training

As you work through your first textbook or course, you may find that creating flashcards is much more exciting and easier than actually doing them. Watching pages turn while we advance to more topics is highly alluring, yet there must be a balance between creating and doing the exercises.

We prefer to think of Anki exercises as training rather than review. Review is something a high school or college student commonly endures to get a high grade on a upcoming test. But we aren't reviewing through Anki. We are learning through Anki. If we can't recall the word or recognize it during conversation, we haven't truly learned it yet. In Anki, we are training ourselves to improve our language skill every day by recalling more and more words faster and training ourselves to understand more of the spoken and written language.

Think of these Anki sessions as training. The boxer must train his reflexes and punches to be faster and stronger than his opponent. The bodybuilder must hit his weak points as hard as he can to bring perfect balance to his body. Language learners must hit new words, phrases, and grammar points from all angles to fully develop all five of the language skills. Just knowing how to punch, how to bench press, or how to read a new word is not enough.

LEARN FROM WHAT YOU LOVE

There is no point in time where we become ready for material made by native speakers for native speakers. It is certainly not when you complete that set of six French textbooks. This imaginary point in time where we will be magically ready to understand everything doesn't exist. We don't even need to understand half of everything. We just need some simple rules.

You might feel that you haven't mastered the basics after one textbook, and this feeling may definitely reflect some truth. And what about the everyday things in life in French speaking countries: paying bills, renting an apartment, going to the bank, and working at a company? If you would like to live and work abroad one day, a certain set of vocabulary and phrases is going to be needed. You may even wish to purchase an additional coursebook to make sure that you don't sound like another foreigner. Go for it.

Some dedicated language learners find a series of coursebooks and textbooks to be interesting because progression and the learning process itself can be exciting. Every chapter brings new grammar structures that allow the learner to express larger and larger ideas. The beginning months can be highly stimulating and intriguing since everything is new, and coursebooks present these new ideas and grammar structures in a way that is easy to understand.

Some of those in the intermediate stages of a language, however, can testify to what eventually follows after the first few textbooks are completed. Many realize that they still struggle to understand most native material, so they buy more advanced books covering more grammar, phrases, and idioms. They go harder in their learning routine and study for more than three hours per day. These advanced grammar explanations are now long-winded, and new language can be highly situational. And there's always more vocabulary to learn. The first few thousand came easy with a little bit of effort, but now suddenly there's 30,000 that they feel that they are expected to know!

"Fun? There's no time for that. I have to learn more!", may be the last words of your motivation before it disappears. It's so easy to become trapped and confined within a bubble of language learning materials. Learning may unknowingly become stale, boring, and inefficient for months and years.

This book exists to say that you will have a lot more fun and motivation in the long-term when you supplement what you learn from fun things with these language learning materials. Of course, common sense says to do things the other way around. Then again, you have so many hopeful French learners who begin learning and drop out when things becomes too dry and boring.

An Alternative Course

Let's use these advanced resources as references to look up any new or unfamiliar language structures when we encounter them in native materials. Wouldn't it be nice to quickly drop in, understand the gist of the target word or structure, and be done with these resources? Lengthy grammar explanations can easily be forgotten, yet a large context from a story that we truly care about can burn in our memory for years. That's the power of context.

You might not even need any advanced textbook. In the age of the internet, quick searches to many questions can provide an accurate answer in just a minute or two. Online dictionaries can provide the basic meaning to an overwhelming majority of words and phrases and give plenty of example sentences. If more explanation is desired, internet searches for target sentence structures will reveal resources that can provide sufficient explanations to most structures.

When you switch your primary learning source from coursebooks to native materials, it's recommended that you keep adding to your original Anki deck. There will probably be a backlog of hundreds of new cards that you have created but have not been tested on yet. This information is likely to be commonly found in native materials, so let's keep building that strong foundation with the original deck.

When there are already 1000+ Anki cards created from coursebook material, it may take a few days to see the content mined from native materials show up during Anki practice. It may be tempting to start that new deck, but your patience will rewarded. The new content will show up during Anki sessions if you keep your deck order mixed.

For native French materials, we will use the same four Anki exercises: Production, Cloze, Listening, and Shadowing. In order for these exercises to be smooth and engaging, we must wisely choose our sentences from native materials. We will then need to learn the meaning of the new words, phrases, and sentence structures using online dictionaries, internet searches, image searches.

Without Love, All of This Learning Is Meaningless

Let's switch our primary source for learning to French websites, dramas, books, music, or whatever got us interested in the language in the first place. Let this material become your new textbook. Learning from native French materials that you truly love to read, watch, and listen to for fun will help sustain motivation for the long-term.

Foreign pop culture and TV do not have to be the end goal in learning a language. There is so much more to a language than what you might find on TV. Regardless of the language and culture, low-quality TV programs can numb the mind rather than excite it. For sustaining long-term motivation for years, it's best to find a hobby in French that you truly enjoy and can learn from. You will know when you find it. You will stop asking yourself the question, "is this all there is?"

Some folks may just wish to meet, befriend, and be proficient in communicating with people in French. In this case, Facebook, Twitter, and other social platforms provide instant gold mines of sentences and passages to dissect. You can bring these written words to life using text-to speech programs and hear surprisingly somewhat natural renditions of them performed by automated speakers.

You may also find new topics to read up on through social media. Make French speaking friends. Press the "Like" button on new pages. Join French groups that pique your interest. Follow famous people that you admire. These actions will immerse your social feed in only your target language.

If what you truly enjoy is found only in reading materials, so be it. Some of the world's most impressive polyglots claim a strong habit of extensive reading is one of the secrets to their amazing abilities. Shadowing is not required, and the other three Anki exercises can still provide a well-rounded practice session.

It is common advice to listen to the target language daily or as often as possible for listening comprehension practice, but try asking yourself this question with each material. Would this audio or visual material add enjoyment to your life or not? The answer is easy to figure out. If it takes more than two seconds to answer yes, it's no.

Two Passages Is Enough

Blogs, comics, books, websites, movies, and TV programs all contain these juicy sentences to break down and learn. If you have ever tried to study any of these materials diligently in the past, however, you know how enormous a task it can be. How do we focus long enough to break down an entire online article or even a short story line by line? How do we not become overwhelmed by websites where everything is in French? How can we study a TV drama?

How do we keep up the willpower to continue these unsustainable study routines after just two days? The problem gets worse and worse. We burn all initial motivation pushing ourselves to break down and learn massive amounts of language until the day comes when we would rather do anything but another day of routine study.

Let's now revisit the method discussed in the first chapter but this time go into more detail. Immerse yourself in the French material that you love without any English assistance for roughly 20 minutes. As you carefully read, watch, and listen, identify the words unknown to you and that are repeated multiple times.

Quickly write down the unknown words that are repeated two or more times and continue without looking anything up in the dictionary nor stopping the reading, video, or audio. Include the page numbers, video times, audio track times, and screenshots for reference later.

After the 20 minutes or so have passed, pick just two small passages that you are highly interested in learning. For the purposes of this book, one passage can be a single long sentence, a few sentences, or even brief dialogues (two to three lines or even more). There is no need to translate entire online articles or drama episodes when looking for these sentences and passages. We don't want to burn ourselves out from over-extending our desire to learn too quickly. A few sentences each day along with fun, immersion, and consistency are key.

There is an amazing process that slowly blooms as you read, listen, and mine a single topic for sentences. When you mine passages over and over from a particular subject matter for weeks and months, you will come to know its most commonly used words and phrases. Once you have a strong grasp on the high frequency words, you will be able to piece together more and more of the meaning of new content from that source as you first hear or see it.

When new words and phrases come from a much larger story or plot that you are highly interested in, all that new information becomes so much more memorable. Almost every line has character to it, and they can become unforgettable. It's the power of context.

Forget the Rest!

Listen, watch, or read as you normally do in English. Watch videos and read materials once or twice and no more. Don't watch the same video, movie, or TV episode over and over until you break down everything from it for the sake of learning. That's no fun at all. What might be more fun is exploring the near endless amount of native French material available online. Learning just a few lines of dialogue from each episode or chapter is enough to move on to the next one.

That last line is so vital to making all of this learning fun, so we would like to repeat it. Learning just a few words or lines of dialogue from each episode or chapter is enough to move on to the next one.

But why two passages and not three passages? Each passage does require a significant amount of work. The process of breaking down and learning the sentences, looking up new words, searching for answers to potential questions we might have, and creating the Anki cards takes a good chunk of time. Two can take from anywhere from 45 minutes to two hours (including the immersion time) depending on how curious you are and the speed you work at. For the sake of consistency, two is recommended, but three is definitely possible as well.

French Is Not Too Fast

Using English subtitles to watch French TV shows, movies, dramas, and videos is an English reading activity with some background noise. You will learn nothing outside a few basic words. You might be tempted to use them to help you focus on the story or relax after an intense study session, but if you choose to use them, native speakers will always talk too fast for you.

They will always talk too fast unless you take the time each and every day to practice trying to comprehend what they mean. But how can you comprehend them in the beginner and intermediate stages when they use thousands of words that you don't know yet? Listening comprehension is a skill that is built through practicing with whatever vocabulary that you do know at the time and relying on context for the words that you do not know.

You will understand the foreign language only by consistently trying to understand the foreign language. Anki exercises are amazingly helpful, but you need every chance that you can get to build towards your reading and listening abilities. Some people like to cite that it takes roughly 10,000 hours of practice to achieve a high level of skill in anything, and this number may or may not be completely accurate. The value of consistent practice, however, is something most of us can agree on.

Listening comprehension is arguably the weakest skill of the average language learner, for most instruction of foreign languages is provided through text or explanations in the learner's native tongue. While audio tracks accompanying language courses are certainly helpful, you may quickly find that they do not provide the volume of practice necessary to understand native speakers out in the everyday world.

While subtitles in French are extremely helpful to learning key moments from video materials, it's poison to our listening comprehension ability. Sadly, these subtitles don't come equipped with the native speakers that you encounter in the real world. So, let's turn these subtitles off, too. They are a French reading exercise, which is definitely an improvement over an English one, but we will get plenty of that later in the Cloze exercises and while freely reading native French materials.

We don't have a French mommy and daddy to speak to us every day for 8-12 hours for 10+ years. You can pay tutors to do just that, but that becomes expensive to do every day for even one hour a day. Without these adult native speakers constantly around, your ears remain incredibly weak. Listening to native materials every day and regularly doing the Anki exercises will help to alleviate this problem.

If you would like to learn French from music, song lyrics would be an exception to this no subtitle rule. Singing the correct lyrics is already a difficult endeavor in our native language, and mishearing lyrics is just as common as it is funny. Start with the lyrics and make it a game to work your way towards relying less and less on them. If you don't want to sing and would rather just listen, you are missing a huge opportunity to improve your pronunciation, remember new words, and have quite a lot of fun.

No Subtitles, But How?

If there are irremovable English subtitles in a video, we can block them from view by cutting out and placing a wide and thick but short piece of paper in front of our computer screens. You won't need the subtitles and transcripts until you have found your passages for learning but until then train your ears to find the words that are both unknown to you and that are repeated frequently. The moments that you desire to understand the most can also become one of your passages for the day. Simply jot down the video time for later reference and don't press pause.

Keeping English subtitles out can be fairly difficult for some folks. You will be tested. You will need determination and faith to fight against the habit of doing everything in English. If allowed even for a brief moment, you feed the idea that you must understand everything to get the most enjoyment from the material. This idea, however, is not necessarily true when you consider the enjoyment you gain as you gradually notice yourself being able to understand more and more each and every day. Seeing true progress in yourself is a powerful emotion. It is self-empowering.

Start by watching and reading things where the premise is easily understandable. You may want to first choose material that you have seen before, so you can get used to everything being in French while still being able to follow the plot. Despite how good it may be for listening practice, it can be maddening watching the same episode or movie five or more times. Watch and read how you normally would in your native language. Once or twice is sufficient.

Work towards building and maintaining a habit of freely reading, listening, and watching without stopping. Do not continually stop to look up words and phrases. Do not look up anything at all until the brief immersion period ends. Trying new material and getting lost quickly is frustrating, but when you do possess something that you personally find exciting and can understand the gist, it's enough. When you finally realize that you do not need to understand everything said and can still enjoy your favorite material, you will know victory.

Choose Easy

At the end of the immersion time, you'll have a list of scribbled words, video times, and page numbers to review, but some of these potential passages could be too difficult for your current level. If you select contexts with four or more unknown words altogether, it's still possible to break down all the vocabulary and grammar. Yet when these difficult passages are repeatedly selected, so many new words, phrases, and grammar points can raise numerous questions to look up and make the learning process slow-paced and tedious.

These types of passages can lead to frustrating Cloze and Shadowing exercises. Shadowing becomes a nuisance when there are too many new words and too much unfamiliar language. Our tongues will seemingly freeze up when the difficulty bar is set too high. During a Cloze exercise, we won't be able to figure out the missing word if there are too many unfamiliar words in the context. These kinds of exercises can cause your interest to wane and take the enjoyment out of Anki practice.

Choosing easy can make learning so much more fun and even addictive. Choosing contexts with just one, two, or three new words allows learning to happen seemingly at a faster pace. When the level of the challenge before us is at just the right level, we can enter a flow-like state where our learning becomes much more pleasurable and satisfying.

Where to Find French Subtitles

Obtaining the subtitles and transcripts for specific audio and video materials is not always possible. Yet once they are in our hands, learning straight from the material that you love becomes possible.

Although somewhat limited, Netflix (*https://www.netflix.com*) does offer some French TV shows and movies with French subtitles. In order to access these French subtitles, you will need to change Netflix's language settings to French under "Account" and "My Profile".

If you are looking for something more inspirational and uplifting, TED Talks in French can be found on YouTube as well by searching YouTube for "Ted Talks français". And if you are interested in news, politics, and foreign affairs, Euronews (*http://fr.euronews.com*) provides news coverage via video along with full transcripts.

Searching the internet for "French subtitles" will net you all kinds of interesting ideas to try out. For example, the website Simpsons Park (*http://www.simpsonspark.com*) offers French transcripts for episodes of *The Simpsons* dubbed in French. These can be accessed by finding the web page for the episode that you are interested in watching and then clicking "Voir le script de l'épisode en VF".

Double Check Your Work

Once we have broken down the new passages and learned the new words and grammatical information, we will have a far better understanding of their meaning. Understanding the exact meaning behind the words can be tricky from time to time. It can be very easy to miss the underlying tone and hidden connotation in a foreign language, and this becomes more apparent whenever any language is translated. Perhaps you have seen the results of this on photos of funny T-shirts or inappropriately translated signs in Asia. We wouldn't want the same thing to happen to us when we spoke or wrote something, right?

In that case, we should use the English subtitles to double check the meaning that we came up with in our head. Yet this doesn't mean that we should use English subtitles and translations when freely watching and reading French material. After the 20 minutes or so has ended and the passages for learning have been selected, it is OK to check the English subtitles to clarify any underlying tone and meaning in the words. It is highly important to make sure that we completely understand what we are trying to learn before we put it into practice. Language textbooks usually provide English translations for this reason.

All this subtitle and translation talk might sound somewhat contradictory, so here's an easier way to think about it. Native materials are for long and extensive listening and reading practice. Subtitles and translations are for short and intensive learning.

How to Learn Vocabulary Really Fast

Ultimately, you may use the Anki exercises any way that you wish, but here is one way to dissect new material. New words and phrases get one Production and one Listening card. Cloze cards can also be used for some of these words and phrases if additional practice is desired. Otherwise, new or still unfamiliar grammar structures and verb conjugations get one Cloze card. Shadowing gets three cards (Blind Shadowing, Shadowing with English text, and Shadowing with French text).

After those cards have been created, here is where we can take it to the next level and learn thousands of words over time with relative ease. Use online dictionaries like Collins Dictionary to find one or two sample sentences for each of the new words and phrases from the passage. Create Listening cards for these one or two sample sentences. If they contain the new word or phrase plus two or three new words, it will be too difficult. If they contain just one additional new word, however, that is perfect!

Take this additional new word from the sample sentence and create one Production and one Listening card. You could also create a few Cloze cards here if you think there is enough context to work with. Repeat this cycle by finding new sample sentences for new words!

If we learned the phrase "do in advance" from our chosen passage for instance, we can do some work and attack it from several diverse angles. Here are five sample phrases that we might find in the online dictionary or in our grammar book: "do homework in advance", "do prep work in advance", "be ready in advance", "tell her in advance", and "pay rent in advance".

Continue for however long you like. In the end, you will create a ton of Production and Listening cards, and this makes for very simple and fast Anki sessions considering that they are the easier exercises. This is just one way to mine sentences using online dictionaries, yet it is just one amongst the hundreds of possibilities that exists in the age of the internet. We strongly encourage you to explore those possibilities and see what you can find.

FLUENCY IS A HABIT

This final chapter is perhaps the most important one contained in this book. It's a call to action. It requires you the reader to stop passively reading along and to take action. If you don't take action every day towards learning French and doing activities in French, fluency will remain an enigma and forever be outside of your reach. If you want to be really good at French, you have to make it a part of your daily life. Taking steps every single day towards what you desire the most is how you create and maintain new habits.

When it comes to taking action towards creating new habits, however, there is a universal truth that we must face. If it does not get scheduled, it does not get done. We must decide on —and then commit to —a routine that we will follow every day, as faithfully as we can. There must be a very specific time during the day when we will do our passage mining, learning, and Anki training. Otherwise, lesser tasks and distractions sneak in, and the age-old excuse of "I couldn't find the time..." starts coming out of our mouths. That classic excuse signals that we never took the next step to set up a specific time and place.

Go ahead and set a specific time of day when you have 45 to 90 minutes to start on the following routine. Early morning before work or school or right afterward is recommended to make it the most important priority while we have the momentum to get things done.

Sample Starting Schedule

Monday - Two new passages

Tuesday - Two new passages

Wednesday - Two new passages

Thursday - Anki 10 new cards / 10 due cards

Friday - Anki 10 new cards / 10 due cards

Saturday - Anki 10 new cards / 10 due cards

Sunday - Extensive reading / listening

Feel free to play around with this starting schedule and make it your own. This is just merely a template for you to start with and improve upon. Test your own ideas and see what brings the most learning and enjoyment to your own program.

Our brains can be sapped after 45-90 minutes of intensive learning and Anki training, but if you stopped at this point, you would be forgetting a very important piece to gaining fluency. Output in either writing or speaking for at least 20-30 minutes should be a part of your everyday language learning routine. That is the only way that you will ever get faster at expressing your own thoughts and ideas in French. The intensive learning and Anki training will expand upon your understanding of French vocabulary and grammar, but can you express what you are thinking or feeling without asking yourself "how do I say..." every minute? If you have to shrink down Anki sessions or learn just one passage in order to include daily output practice in your routine, do it. All of these activities are equally important.

On Anki training days, it is important to take at least an additional 20-30 minutes each day to read, listen to, and watch material in French like on the passage mining days. This "immersion" habit should become a part of your daily routine as well. We need to train our ears and eyes daily if we desire to hit high levels of proficiency. If you can manage to add both output practice and this extensive reading or listening time to your daily minimum routine, you'll have a very balanced program of input, output, learning, and practice. And you'll also learn extremely fast.

If you are looking to learn full-time, try learning two passages and doing the Anki sessions on the same day. Now, this might take you a little over two hours, so maintaining this level of commitment is only recommended for those feeling extra motivated. Make sure to take some sort of break between these two intensive learning activities. You could do three passages or longer Anki sessions, but switching between these two different activities is recommended to maximize your attention span and enjoyment.

If you are looking to go full immersion in your home environment, it would be wise to keep your intensive learning and Anki sessions under three hours. There comes a point in time during each day where you might find it much more productive to allocate your time to extensive activities rather than more study. Activities such as interacting with native speakers or freely watching and reading native materials with no English can be done as frequently as you like, as they do not require as much focus as intensive learning does.

You may need to take two or even more days off occasionally from both creating Anki exercises and training with them. During this time, do things in the target language for enjoyment alone. Sing French songs. Play some video games in French. Read up on topics in French that interest you. Watch videos, TV shows, and movies with no subtitles. Binge watching is highly encouraged!

During your free time, downtime, and times of relaxation, you always have a choice. Will you do something in your native language or French? Understand that you always have the power to choose. You are not doomed to a habit of doing everything in your native language. It's a particularly tough habit to break after learning to do practically everything in your native language, but it's a habit that can be fought by not just learning French every day but living it.

Lang-8, Italki, and HelloTalk

Production and Shadowing exercises help our speech patterns to sound more native-like while working to reduce our accent, yet we need to practice communicating our own thoughts and make sure other people can comprehend them. Being able to continually talk in French is an impressive feat, yet being understood and grammatically correct all the time is another issue. Sometimes, we will string together words and grammar that make perfect sense in our heads, yet we will be shocked when the listening party tells us that they have no idea what we just said.

Lang-8 *(http://lang-8.com)* is a free language exchange website where users make posts in the language that they wish to practice. You receive corrections in exchange for correcting other people's posts in your native language. Users can write about anything. We can write about what has been on our minds all day or even specific topics that we are interested in. When we correct other people's posts, corrections for our entries come within hours.

In terms of time and money, it may be the most effective way of receiving corrections. It is very convenient to visit the page at any time, write for 10-20 minutes, make a few easy corrections for other users, and leave to go about our day. Later during the same day, we can return to find the corrections and make sure that we never forget them. How? Create Anki exercises.

If you are willing to pay a few dollars a session to speak with tutors face to face, Italki *(https://www.italki.com)* may be the better alternative. In order to use Italki, you will need to search for a teacher of your liking, schedule for an available time slot, and be logged on the video-calling software Skype *(https://www.skype.com)* at that time. Good teachers will send you notes of their corrections, so you will still be able to create Anki exercises from what you have learned. Face-to-face conversation and tutoring does have its advantages, so it may be worth the price.

HelloTalk *(https://www.hellotalk.com)* is a highly popular app that has opened new possibilities of language exchange through texting. Most language learners rate this app very positively, as it is possibly the most convenient way to connect directly with native speakers of almost any language that you are interested in learning. It is a great platform to start organic conversations with other users while you make new friends and correct each other as you both progress. Texting certainly takes the pressure off of face to face conversations in meeting new people through new languages, so this may be the choice for you.

Start With 10 / 10 Sessions

Let's clarify a few terms to make the follow discussion easier to understand. Anki practice sessions entails doing new cards (color coded blue in Anki) and review cards (color coded green in Anki under "Due"). New cards are cards that we have created but not yet seen during practice sessions. Review cards have been viewed at least once before. So, 10/10 refers to doing an Anki session with 10 new cards and 10 review cards.

In Anki, you can set the number of exercises to be completed per day to 10/10 or whatever numbers you would like. This can easily be done by opening Anki, clicking on the gear to the right of your deck, and selecting 'Options'. Set 'New cards/day' to 10, and then click the 'Reviews' tab and set 'Maximum reviews/day' to 10. The cards are reviewed in the order that they are made by default, but to make sure that we see a nice medley of different words, phrases, and sentences, shuffling the cards is recommended and also easy to do. In do so, click the 'New cards' tab, look for 'Order', and select 'Show new cards in random order'. These settings should be good enough to start with.

100 "Maximum reviews/day" is the current default setting in Anki at the time of writing this book, but if we keep this setting and complete the entire review every day, Anki practice sessions alone will quickly start exceeding 90 minutes daily. This does not include the time it takes to learn new materials and create cards from them.

Why not be a diligent student and and do all the review cards no matter what it takes? Language learning is not a test. It is a hobby to do in our free time. It should be fun! Exercising, lifting weights, and playing intense sports all have some pain and fatigue involved but also a considerably large amount of endorphins (the 'feel good' chemical) that we can receive in return. Foreign language learning is the same. We must cap pain and fatigue and maximize enjoyment on a daily basis to create a long-term language learning habit.

The starting recommendation is set at 10/10 cards during Anki practice sessions, and a high amount of caution is advised if you would like to increase those numbers. Put on some safety gloves before touching this dangerous electrical current that can easily shock all the motivation out of you. Dividing Anki sessions into small time blocks throughout the day is a wise idea if you are thinking about doing more Anki.

Experiment with your routine. If you want to incorporate more Anki practice, a large number such as 25/25 could potentially be done if broken into two or more different sessions throughout the day. Doing such a large number every day will be a tremendously difficult habit to maintain, but if you are feeling particularly motivated on certain days, go for it. On the days that you don't feel like doing Anki but should do it, do just 10/10 to keep the habit going. You could even do 5/5 cards every day and still have plenty of time to create new cards from new material.

Doing 50+ cards each day can be highly detrimental to our success. More Anki does not mean more learning and progress if it causes your internal fun and motivation meter to plummet and approach zero. Let's stop training for the Agony Olympics and hellish ultra-marathons of needlessly long Anki sessions. You will do exponentially more Anki cards just by doing it consistently as a habit.

Even when we hit our personal goals, we will not run out of new things to learn and practice. Consistency with Anki is what will keep us learning until that point and even past it while we aim at higher goals. To build this consistency with Anki, keep sessions under an hour and don't force yourself to do more for the sake of faster progress. Stop right before you get bored and keep yourself hungry for the next session.

Start with 5/5 sessions if you have trouble focusing during 10/10 sessions. Train to grow stronger in both French proficiency and your ability to focus deeply. A habit of waking up and going straight to social media is highly detrimental to our ability to deeply focus. Start your day with morning walks and inspirational audiobooks to draw your focus away from everything happening around you so that you can focus on everything happening within you.

If for whatever reason you no longer like a card that you created weeks or months ago, it's time to delete that sucker. You may make a few mistakes in creating exercises while testing new ideas and have to delete a large number of cards over time. Do not be discouraged. In fact, we should embrace it as part of the learning process and the learning-about-learning process.

The End

Thank you so much for taking the time to read our book! If the ideas in this book have made learning fluent French more accessible to you, at least a little, why not show your support by sharing this book with a friend or even writing an Amazon review? Take a minute to write about what you liked and disliked, and your suggestions might make it into the next edition.

Made in the USA
Middletown, DE
29 December 2017